Formation Team, British Championships, Blackpool, England. 1987.

Master of Ceremonies, Ohio Star Ball, Columbus, Ohio. 1986.

BALLROOM

Photographs by
Ken Graves and Eva Lipman

Text by Sally Sommer

MILKWEED EDITIONS

SEEING DOUBLE SERIES OF COLLABORATIVE BOOKS

Ballroom

© 1989. Photographs by Eva Lipman and Ken Graves
© 1989. Text by Sally Sommer
All rights reserved.
Printed in 1989 by Milkweed Editions
Post Office Box 3226
Minneapolis, MN 55403
Books may be ordered from the above address.

93 92 91 90   4 3 2 1

We are grateful for the generous sponsorship of *Ballroom* by Sage and
John Cowles.

Major support for the "Seeing Double Collaborative Book Series" has
been provided by the Bush Foundation.

This and other Milkweed Editions books are made possible in part by
grants provided by the Cowles Media Foundation, the Dayton Hudson
Foundation for Dayton's and Target Stores, First Bank Systems Founda-
tion, the Jerome Foundation, the Literature Program of the National
Endowment for the Arts, and the Minnesota State Arts Board, through an
appropriation by the Minnesota State Legislature. The Minnesota State
Arts Board received additional funds to support this activity from the
National Endowment for the Arts. Milkweed Editions is the recipient of a
McKnight Foundation Award administered by the Minnesota State Arts
Board.

Library of Congress Catalog Number: 89-36395

ISBN 0-915943-44-1

Library of Congress Cataloging-in-Publication Data

Graves, Ken, 1942-
    Ballroom : photographs / by Ken Graves and Eva Lipman.
        p.   cm.
    ISBN 0-915943-44-1
    1. Ballroom dancing—Pictorial works. 2. Dance photography.
I. Lipman, Eva. II. Title.
GV1746.G74   1989   89-36395
793.3'3—dc20   CIP

This project was completed with the support of a National Endowment
for the Arts Fellowship.

In memory of Mitchell Payne,
photographer and colleague,
and Paul Cahill, dance teacher
and best friend.

Acknowledgments

by Ken Graves and Eva Lipman

This body of photographs reflects our efforts as visual artists. Also represented here is the generosity of those individuals who made it possible for us to realize this project fully. Special thanks to John Kimmins, Larry Dean, Vic Dominic, Frank Allen, and Ricky Geiger who made easier our passage into this world. We thank Sam Sodano who had the special gift of making us feel welcome, and Judi Hatton, an individual spirit, whose support came from a shared interest in making this subculture visible through our photographs. We are grateful to Craig Gordan, Vicki Genovese, Lance Sexton, Melinda Maudlin and Sharon McGraw for opening their doors to a stranger with a camera. The efforts on our behalf by Carol Coleman, Esther Don, and Alan Feuer deserve mention. Our friends from England, who welcomed us to several children's competitions, were very helpful. Their hospitality and kindness were unmatched, and we are deeply grateful to them.

Here at home, we are most indebted to Efraim, Lara, Ami, Paula and Emily. The existence of this work owes much to their endurance, understanding, and willingness to accept a role in which the work often claimed all our attention. We'd like to thank our parents, Helen and Irving Neuman, Robert and Mildred Graves, and our families, especially Yetta and Isaac, for being so generous, as well as all the friends, teachers and students who over the years have played their part and contributed to a gentler understanding of the human experience, and, we hope, to the realization of that vision in this body of work.

We are indebted to the exceptional staff at Milkweed Editions—to Emilie Buchwald, our editor, and Randy Scholes, the Art Director, whose enthusiasm and commitment to the making of beautiful books made this volume possible. Thanks are due to Kitty Haupt, who received and typed our rewrites over and over again with untiring patience. We thank our writer, Sally Sommer, who spent hours with us editing and organizing the photographs, and generously lent her dance expertise to the text.

Most especially, we thank our dear, close friend Jennifer Ford, whose unfailing dedication to her dancing was an inspiration throughout. And finally, no acknowledgment can omit our debt to the dancers who are the subject of this book. Guided by our intuition, we identified with their obsession, and their energy, which left us breathless.

by Sally Sommer

I would like to thank Brooks McNamara for battering down the barriers that separate high art and popular forms, and Alan Lomax for connecting dance to the streams of life. Larry Schultz and Sandra Cameron have given unfailing help and generosity. My gratitude to Al Minns, whose love of dancing and artistry set standards of excellence for us all.

BALLROOM

Photographers' Preface

Camera artists have traditionally explored subjects in quiet isolation, suspicious of another photographer's presence. To share a subject with another, in a tight space, is rare. It requires releasing a hold on the prize.

Prior to meeting at a ballroom dance competition in Florida, we were photographing dancers independently. Our respect for each other's photographs was immediate, and developed into a collaborative effort. We began to see the photographs as a single body of work. Our efforts became unified, the failures and triumphs shared. We were both teachers and students on a journey through a fantasy world. We laid open our photographic proofs just as if we were entrusting someone else with the care of a personal diary. Our technical errors, vulnerabilities and hesitations were exposed. We had to permit one another to fail, as well as to succeed. Like children returning home, weary from combing the neighborhoods on Halloween night, we sorted through our findings looking for treasures. And, in strong light, the goods were edited into a variety of delights.

What guided us while working was often as mysterious as the direction taken by a wind-up toy. We would move forward, muse, and backtrack, always in a state of readiness. Our cameras tugged on our bodies. During this odyssey, our process was one of selecting from the public sphere.

The attraction of ballroom dancing as a photographic subject was rooted in a long-time fascination with lives lived out at the extreme end of human experience. The competitive dancer's will to succeed left little room in this drama for compromise or apathy. To be the best, nothing less than total immersion would do. Identifying with the obsession and dedication was exhilarating. The ballroom event was our entry into a magical kingdom, unfamiliar and extraordinary. Every event was inflated: self-consciously and deliberately imbued with elegance and style. Appearance was held sacred. Here, indeed, was life puffed up. Although our senses were stimulated and sharpened by the spectacle, it was always the potential of what could be, the mystery about to reveal itself, which held our imaginations.

It was on the periphery of the dance floor where we found our most compelling imagery. Backstage was an open space filled with promise and surprise. Everywhere were pockets of activity, where the popular conception of contrivance would falter. Between competitions, elegance was permitted to relax. It was in these darker recesses of the ballroom that tensions were played out. Dancers paced and stretched like runners, before setting themselves in their assigned lanes, their energy held in check. Preparations were made for transforming themselves into creatures of magic and flight. Make-up was anchored to faces, and women, like exotic birds resting during a migratory flight, sat enveloped in billowing gowns. Their partners' bodies seemed held up by the rigid cut of their tuxedos.

Our interest extended to photographing society balls, and sprang from a need to see more. These couples' movements were unrestrained, flirtatious and seductive. Touch dancing was filled with expressions of human need. Witnessing this pleasure was cathartic for us, and provided a needed balance to the artifice and strict discipline in which the ritual of competitive dancing had immersed us. These social events were our last stop on this visual journey, and cushioned our re-entry into a reality at once more familiar and ordinary.

Our aim as artists was neither to idealize the dancer nor the dance, nor to show the world of ballroom at its best or worst. We tried, rather, to find the universal in the particulars of the event. Our interest was to reveal surprise, to secure the unguarded moments, to record those instances that exist for each of us when we think no one is looking. We expressed, unconsciously, like many artists, our personal vision of reality. For us, individually and together, the question was—what could we bring to this subject? These photographs, we believe, answer that question.

1

Competition

Competition

Locked in an embrace, a man and woman twirl in a world between fantasy and reality. These are competition ballroom dancers, graceful angels who serve the god of dance. Suspended between past and present, they trace elegant configurations on the dance floor which have been distilled from ancient rituals of courtship, now shaped into abstract motions.

Ballroom competitors are virtuosic movers whose fluid revolutions only vaguely resemble what real people do on the dance floor. Holding their bodies high and light, using a complicated vocabulary of gestures and steps, they attack the movement in a way that immediately identifies them. Splendid dancers, they remind us of what we might have been if we had just practiced.

Because their profession demands religious devotion, the ballroom world has become curiously isolated. Like ballerinas, these dancers must pledge body and heart to their art. Flourishing in studios and competitions throughout the world, these ballroom flowers have survived in a self-contained environment that is self-supporting. At its apex is a network of studios, staffed by teachers and championship coaches who earned their rank by winning national and international ballroom dance contests. Supporting the studios are thousands of students, most of whom take lessons for fun, some of whom are the scrappy competitors who will become the coaches of tomorrow. The ecosystem is both efficient and closed, and for the last forty-five years, the dancers have been performing for themselves. Separated from the evolutions that were actually taking place in social dancing, ballroom competitors developed a rigorous technique and florid performance style which is so self-referential that you can spot the studio-trained dancer every time.

During the week they gather at the studios, but on the weekends, they celebrate in the ballrooms of slightly seedy hotels. There, in fierce competitions, couples dance against other couples, and they dance to win. The ballroom floor is turned into a battleground, an arena of plain wood rising like an island of simplicity in a sea of over-designed carpets.

Sponsored by ballroom associations throughout the United States, Europe and Japan, competitions are judged according to exacting standards. Divided into successive heats which winnow out the good from the excellent, competitions are an exotic hybrid of art and sports. Only the best become champions; regional winners move up the ladder to national and international competitions. Along the way, each step is monitored by ubiquitous coaches and judges—high priests and priestesses of the ballroom who uphold the standards of steps and styles. Ballroom dancing is governed by unforgiving laws which have been codified in thick, biblical manuals which set down the commandments of "Thou Shalt Do It This Way," and "Thou Shalt Not Do It That Way," prescribing each dance, step-by-step, in excruciating detail.

Since most of the audience for these competitions is made up of family, friends, and other ballroom dancers, these contests have evolved into fantastical rituals danced by the initiated, performed for the devoted. There are special preparations that must be accomplished before one can enter the sacred dancing area. Special clothing must be worn. And, most importantly, the proper physical actions must be performed with love and exactitude.

This world is the subject of Eva Lipman's and Ken Graves' photographs. Going behind the movements of the dance, they discovered the world of the dancers. Their images capture the mystery of the shadowy world behind the ballroom, pulling taut the tensions between the slick surface of performance and the realities that lie beneath.

The ballroom is a microcosm that reflects the larger world and its truths. Although ballroom competitions are contests of emotional and physical endurance, the subtext is about the impossible pursuit of perfection. This is what we admire. In this mirror we see the deepest truth of the human spirit.

British Championships, Winter Garden, Blackpool, England. 1987.

Classique du Montréal, Canada. 1985.

Practice, Cherry Hill, New Jersey. 1987.

Starlight Room, Cherry Hill, New Jersey. 1986.

Arthur Murray Competition, McGaffee, New Jersey. 1987.

Marc Ballroom Exhibition, New York, New York. 1985.

2

Fantasy

Fantasy

Bending forward, then backward, they let their heads drop to their chests, then throw them back in ecstasy. This is the warm-up, that ritual of preparation shared by all dancers. More than a physical action, the warm-up is a meditation. The pace is deliberate, languid even. As the dancers move from one position to the next, the hypnotic repetition of familiar motion soothes the mind. The focus turns inward, eyes close or stare off contemplatively as they listen to the silent language of muscle and cartilage. Travelling in deep interior space, the dancers make the transition from everyday life to the world of performance. They are vulnerable, throats exposed as if for sacrifice, pliant bodies curved over an invisible altar.

Feathers have become a mainstay of competition *couture*, and dressed in their feathery gowns, the women look like a flock of preening birds. Hems float with plumage in day-glo colors, bodices glitter with rhinestones, sleeves are cut to look like great wings. Although no official regulations exist about costume beyond having to make the feet visible, all the dresses basically look much alike—except for their varying colors and individual sleeve designs. One reason for this similarity is that aspiring champions *always* dress like last year's champions, as if that gives them a guarantee of this year's victory. Since most dresses are made by a few costume designers in England and Canada, the same pattern gets copied again and again. For the modern or smooth-dancing division (the Foxtrot, Tango, Quickstep, Waltz, and Viennese Waltz), a dress will cost between one and two thousand dollars, while a costume for the Latin competition (Cha-cha-cha, Paseo Doble, Rhumba, Samba, Jive), displaying a maximum of skin and a minimum of cloth, may cost slightly less.

In truth, the costumes look as if they were taken from an Astaire and Rogers film, proving that the ties which bind ballroom dance to popular entertainment are still strong.

At one time ballroom dance was queen of the stage and no Broadway show was complete without introducing some stylish new social dance to the public. In vaudeville and nightclubs, sleek couples showed folks how they *might* be able to dance if they took lessons. Since most of these couples also ran studios, the message was clear: Sign up at my studio and you can be king and queen of the ballroom.

But it was Vernon and Irene Castle, undisputed royalty of the ballroom world, who best illustrated how this cozy alliance between stage and studio might be exploited. Elegant and indefatigable, Vernon and Irene dressed like millionaires and danced like angels, twirling across America and Europe in hundreds of dance exhibitions. Because they were beautiful, they left behind them thousands of people who longed to look and dance just like them—which allowed Vernon and Irene to parlay the Castle style into a major industry. They were media stars whose pronouncements were commandments. They sold lessons and how-to booklets, renamed dances in their honor, endorsed everything from corsets to soap and made millions in the process, until their reign abruptly ended with Vernon's untimely death in 1918.

Then, in the early 1930s, their crown passed to the brilliant team of Fred Astaire and Ginger Rogers. The incomparable magic of their partnership, and their larger-than-life images on the silver screen, shaped ideals about dance and romance—which helped prepare the way for the opening of the Fred Astaire Dance Studios in 1947. Middle and lower class America gained hope from the Astaire/Rogers films. No matter how elegant, Fred and Ginger were simple folk, just like the audience. No matter how bad the problem, dancing cured it. Dance paved the way to success. Dance was available to the most ordinary person. Through dance, one achieved fame and fortune. Most importantly, Astaire and Rogers' insouciant charm convinced everyone that ballroom dancing made one elegant and glamorous.

Of all the mythologies of the ballroom, Fred and Ginger's is our most treasured. It is what keeps the students coming to the studios and sustains the competitors in their difficult profession. And is any metaphor of romance more beautiful than the image of Ginger Rogers draped over Fred Astaire's arm, her fluent back arched, frozen in a moment of swooning delirium.

Backstage, Columbus, Ohio. 1986.

Imperial Society, Cherry Hill, New Jersey. 1988.

Imperial Society, Cherry Hill, New Jersey. 1988.

Imperial Society, Cherry Hill, New Jersey. 1988.

Classique du Montréal. 1988.

Classique du Montréal. 1988.

Woman trying on gowns, Ohio Star Ball, Columbus, Ohio. 1986.

Imperial Society, Cherry Hill, New Jersey. 1988.

3

Grooming

Grooming

In ancient times dancer/warriors wore masks to transform themselves into sacred animals or vengeful gods. The masks liberated them from the bonds of self, making them greater than human. Now blush and mascara are the tools of transformation, a thin veneer of color is the mask. Dancers no longer become fearsome gods. Instead, they are smiling puppets with manicured nails and immovable hairdos that testify to the enduring strength of hair spray.

In place of the torn mouths of Tragedy and Comedy, we have the smile. Since ballroom competitors must be able to repeat the same dance in the same way, round after round, reactions and interactions have been choreographed so that the same smile will always flash with the same step. Smiles aren't aimed at the partner, but at the judges and audiences, or maybe they are simply thrown out in space. Latin competitors wink, gasp, and bite the air in passion, frown, and then inexplicably switch emotions and dazzle with a bewildering variety of smiles. Modern competitors wear beatific smiles that should ideal-

ly accompany daydreams. Ambitious competitors are coached on how to turn it on. There are "E-e-e-e" smiles, pretty "Oo-oo-oo-o" pouts and the wide-open "Ah-ah-ah-a-a!" Of all the peculiar performance conventions, the locked-on smile is the most unsettling because it contradicts the very thing these dances are supposed to represent: the romantic connection between man and woman. In big-time competitions, the emotional tone is heated, sweat seeps through make-up and clothes and the disparity between the hard work and the smile becomes more obvious.

But in those moments before the battle, the dancers anoint each other with the holy scepters of combs and make-up. Faces are clear and innocent before the mask is set. A man waits for the touch of the brush, a woman opens her mouth for the soft cream of lipstick. Partnerships are cemented by touch and, for a second competitive animosities are quieted. These are the soft moments before the heat of battle when grooming is a tenderness.

Grooming, U.S. Ballroom Championships, Miami Beach, Florida. 1987.

Latin Formation Team, Blackpool, England. 1988.

Backstage, U.S. Ballroom Championships, Miami, Florida. 1987.

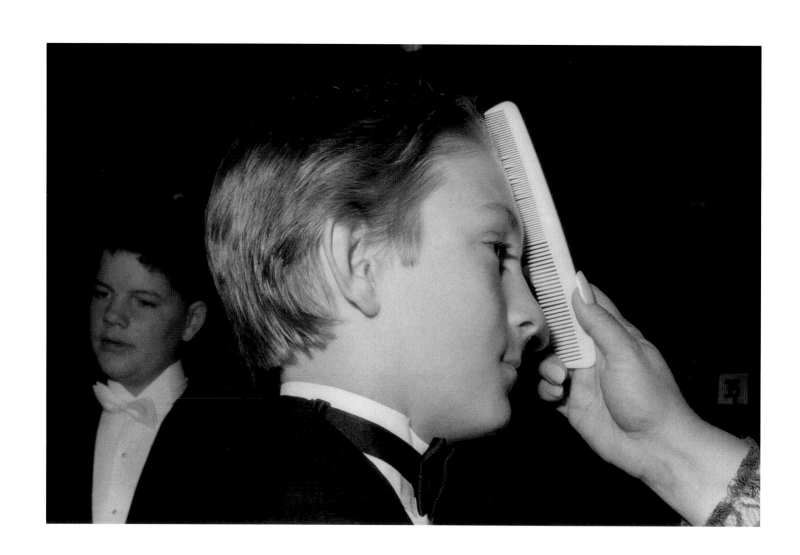

Child Competitor, Miami Beach, Florida. 1987.

Maria and Jennifer, Cherry Hill, New Jersey. 1986.

Northcoast Championships, Cleveland, Ohio. 1987.

Practice Session, Florida State Championships, Palm Beach, Florida. 1987.

Imperial Society, Cherry Hill, New Jersey. 1987.

U.S. Ballroom Championships, Miami Beach. 1987.

Children's Competition, Borehamwood, England. 1988.

Modern Formation Team from Germany, Blackpool, England. 1988.

4

Waiting

Waiting

They wait. The heats are over. Hovering between terror and hope, they cling to each other as they wait for the judges' decisions to be announced. Emotions are raw. They pray, "Let it be me." Or maybe they sleep, or smoke, or stretch.

Waiting is at the heart of competition. They wait for planes, trains and buses, and for competitions to begin. They wait between rounds, and worst of all, they wait for pronouncements that could alter their lives. Just as in the pitched battles of life and death that ballroom competitions imitate, the emotional rhythms swing between fright and boredom.

Competitors stay, they say, because it is an addiction whose rewards—except for the few who make it—are the physical and mental highs. Life is lived at the edge. Competition spices experience, it focuses ambition, and within that inner world are friends hooked on the same dance drug. Many older women are attracted to ballroom dance—and why not? They engage in regular physical exercise with attentive, younger men who treat them well and hold them close when they teach them dancing.

Well-tuned athletes, ballroom dancers spend most of their time training. A minimum of fifteen to twenty hours a week is spent perfecting a routine that will take one-and-a-half minutes to perform. Because there are twelve couples in each round (six couples will make the final heat), and only one-and-a-half minutes of dancing, adjudicators have approximately *ten seconds* of observation time for each couple.

For those who thrive on risk, it's a thrilling gamble, a heady crap shoot with luck: will one emerge a winner or a loser? But, the competitors also add, it takes a savvy blend of artistry and politics to walk away a champion. Stakes are high for the winners, because they will be able to earn good money through coaching and running successful studios.

Of course, what really draws them to the dance is the feeling of two bodies moving together in an embrace, following each other in lyrical rushes of motion. The art of ballroom technique lies in the ability to abandon the body to the ever-shifting responsibilities of leading and following. The fine dancer does not respond to the pressure of a hand or to verbal instructions, but tunes in to the silent language of the partner. Interior signals pass from one body to another like electrical charges. Subtle contractions and flexions in the muscles foretell a shift in weight and direction. This close moving goes beyond cause and effect to something more like simultaneous response. Researchers of mother/infant interactions claim this almost-simultaneous *pas de deux* is our first and most important dance. Perhaps couple dancing is an attempt to recapture that mystical experience.

Good technicians can follow their partners with eyes closed and still be fully accountable for their own weight. This is an unique physical symbiosis of democratic and equal motion. One surrenders to the physicality of the moment as in the act of lovemaking, the model for the graceful duet of couples dancing.

Imperial Society, Cherry Hill, New Jersey. 1987.

British Championships, Blackpool, England. 1988.

Spectator, U.S. Ballroom Championships, Miami Beach, Florida. 1987.

Professional Modern Competitors, Blackpool, England. 1988.

Ohio Star Ball, Columbus, Ohio. 1986.

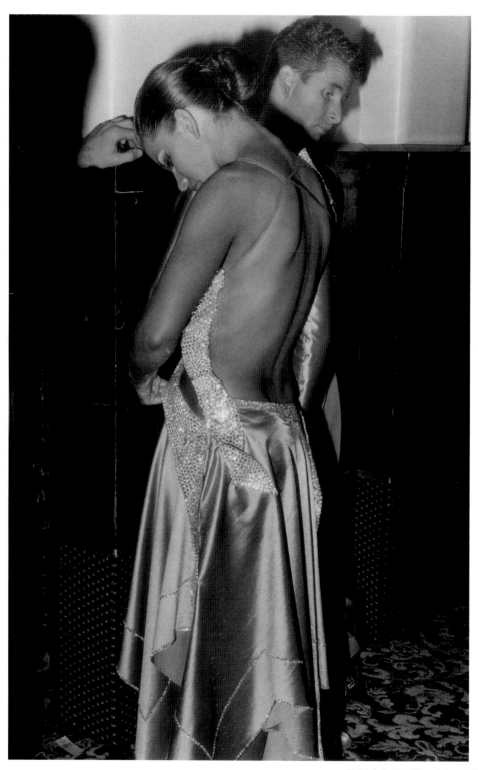

British Latin Champions, Blackpool, England. 1988.

Competitor and Judge, Miami Beach, Florida. 1987.

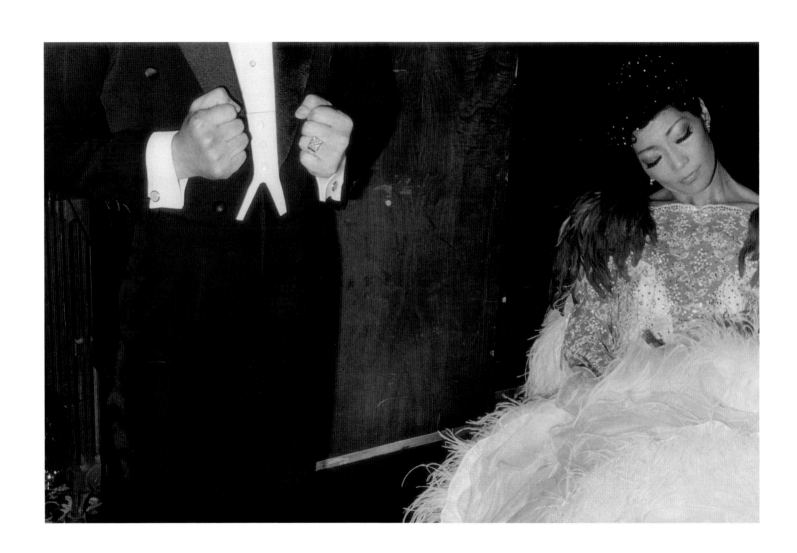

British Championships, Blackpool, England. 1988.

Virginia State Championships, Arlington, Virginia. 1987.

Professional Amateur Division, Arlington, Virginia. 1987.

Imperial Society, Cherry Hill, New Jersey. 1987.

Arthur Murray Competition, Cherry Hill, New Jersey. 1987.

Instructor and Student, Palm Beach, Florida. 1987.

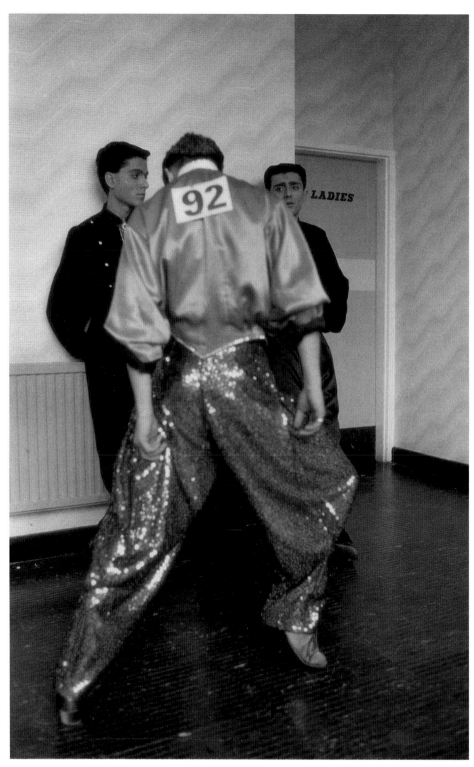

Western European Competitors, Rowstenstahl, England. 1988.

Arthur Murray Competition, Stamford, Connecticut. 1987.

5

Stillness

Stillness

Dancers observing dancers are alert animals arrested in the midst of motion. Because dance is passed from person to person, it is essential they be able to scrutinize and absorb the smallest details of movement and gesture. There is science in their craft and, even as they watch, these skillful technicians are splicing together exotic genes of diverse movement to form a new, recombinant DNA of dance. Sitting in utter stillness, muscles fired for dancing on a deep kinetic level, these ardent voyeurs perform tiny internal tangos, partnering in their imaginations other dancers on the floor.

Unconsciously graceful, they rest in impeccable postures of flawless repose. Magnificent robots, they compute what they are seeing, incorporating tiny bytes of information into their personal programs. They look beyond enjoyment, measuring themselves against what they see, calculating points, taking cues, consuming their competitors' souls.

U.S. Ballroom Championships, Miami, Florida. 1987.

Fred Astaire Competition, Hilton Hotel, New York City. 1983.

Judges and Attendant, Ohio Star Ball. 1986.

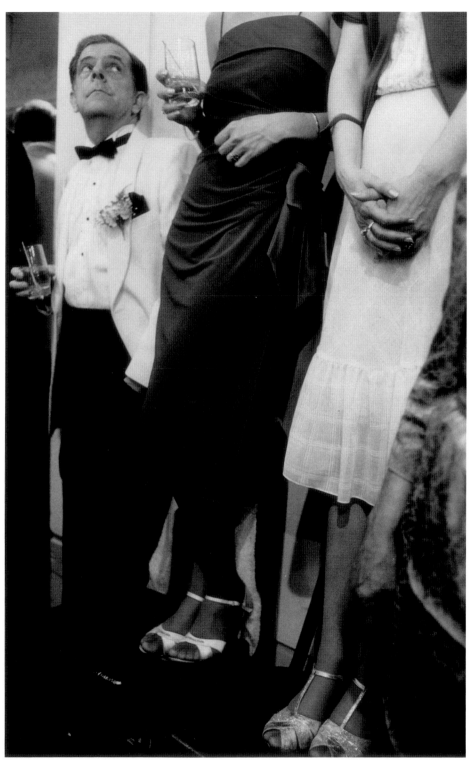

Spectators, Arthur Murray Competition, Cherry Hill, New Jersey. 1986.

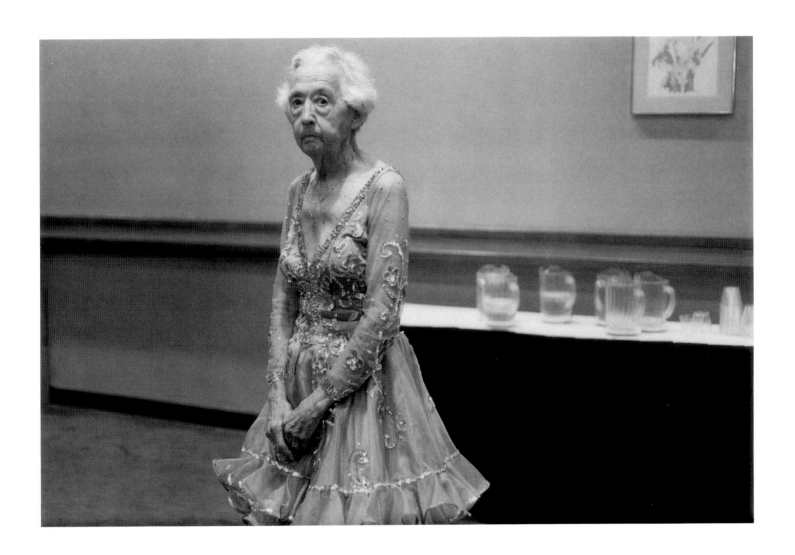

Student Competitor, Cleveland, Ohio. 1987.

Imperial Society, Cherry Hill, New Jersey. 1987.

Imperial Society, Cherry Hill, New Jersey. 1987.

Competitors, U.S. Ballroom Championships. 1987.

Competitors, U.S. Ballroom Championships. 1987.

Competitors, U.S. Ballroom Championships. 1987.

Competitor, British Championships, Blackpool, England. 1988.

Imperial Society, Cherry Hill, New Jersey. 1987.

U.S. Ballroom Championships, Miami Beach, Florida. 1987.

Competitor, Virginia State Championships, Arlington, Virginia. 1987.

6

Children

Children

Cast as adults, children are meant to be complimentary replicas of the grown-ups around them. Imitation, after all, implies adulation.

The child-competitor is an odd creation of an adult fantasy. Grownups venerate themselves by having children copy adult activities—and this early practice prepares the child to be an adult. Yet children locked in a closed-couple embrace, spinning across the floor, are innocents caught in an adult flirtation. They haven't experienced the longing of the romantic love which is the subject of their dance, and, as performers, they are removed from the emotional content of their art. Sexuality is banished from the dance. The mysteries of the world have been disarmed. Left to go through the well-rehearsed motions of the dance, these children become well-behaved objects preoccupied with technique, striving to please the grown-ups who watch.

Children touch us. Beneath the thin veneer of technique, we notice their vulnerabilities—the little protruding tummies, the slightly hunched shoulders, the dazed looks and unsure placement. And we love them more because they are not perfect.

There is, however, a very practical reason for the children to begin training early. Just as in the ballet, years are needed to master the formidable ballroom technique. Hours spent in the classroom will smooth away their technical imperfections, years in junior competitions will toughen their emotions. Many champions began dancing as youngsters, because it can take a lifetime to shape body and mind to the stern discipline of this craft.

But what goes through the child's mind? Does she know she is entering a make-believe world where she must perform old-fashioned dances in slightly out-of-date costumes? Does he view it like a swimming match with physical challenges to be conquered?

Sequence Dancing, Children's Competition, Borehamwood, England. 1988.

Children's Competition, Borehamwood, England. 1988.

Children Competitors, Birmingham, England. 1988.

Children's Competition, Old Tyme, Borehamwood, England. 1988.

Couple #69, Children's Competition, Borehamwood, England. 1988.

Children's Competition, Borehamwood, England. 1988.

Western European Competition, Rowstenstahl, England. 1988.

Children's Competition, Sequence Dancing, Borehamwood, England. 1988.

Children's Competition, Sequence Dancing, Borehamwood, England. 1988.

7

Real Life

Real Life

In real life, ballroom forms are broken. Bodies carelessly twined around each other are beautiful because emotion, not technique, shapes the tangled limbs, the tilt of a head. These men and women, soft and tousled, are attentive to nothing beyond the circle of their private *pas de deux*. Love is not symmetrical. They look at each other, hold each other. The sensuality that was absent on the floor is palpable in their embraces, and they abandon themselves, unmindful of their mussy form. The woman is not responsible for her own weight, the man does not lead her. Cradled by caring hands, they simply curve their bodies together in a tender shape of love.

* * *

Looking at ballroom dancing closely and comparing its art to life, we recognize how the relationship between a man and woman is formalized and reflected in the conventions of ballroom partnering. Stepping back, we discern still deeper meanings. The closed-couple dance is familiar and attractive to us because we long to do it too. We seek the warmth of touch, the solace of one body holding another. The embrace, which is the central physical metaphor of ballroom dancing, reminds us of the essential embrace of life. It is an abstract rendering of that first moment of attachment between infant and mother—a moment which cannot be remembered, yet is never forgotten, because it propels the adult's life-search for a mate.

Dancing abstracts primal actions into formal patterns and shapes social interactions into elegant configurations. Social dance is more than ornamental. It heightens everyday behaviors into dance, and is as necessary as what it mirrors. Its subject is nothing less than human survival, where the seductive foreplay of male and female which assures our perpetuation as a species is celebrated with eloquent motions and special music.

Why do we care about dance? Because the dance and the dancers touch us. What they do, and how well they do it, are relevant. The greater their artistry, the better we love them. For a few moments, the dancer becomes our emissary in an important celebration of life, performing a ritual of affirmation whose choreography has been distilled from the interactions that bind us together. And, through their excellence, the dancers honor us.

Café Society, New York City. 1989.

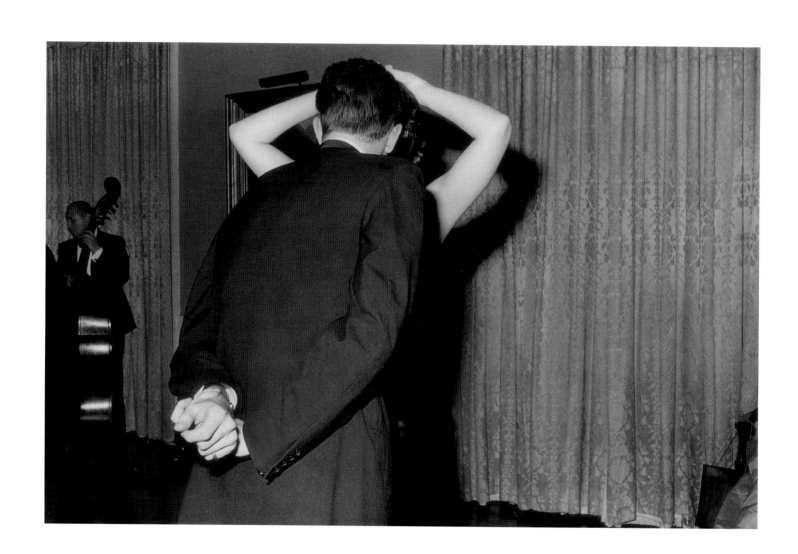

Quadrille Alumni Ball, New York City. 1988.

Quadrille Alumni Ball, New York City. 1988.

General Dancing, Cherry Hill, New Jersey. 1987.

Vienna In Spring, New York City. 1988.

General Dancing, Palm Beach, Florida. 1987.

Russian Nobility Ball, Waldorf Astoria, New York City. 1988.

General Dancing, Kansas City, Missouri. 1987.

Quadrille Masked Ball, New York City. 1989.

Quadrille Ball, New York City. 1989.

Bachelors' Ball, Newport, Rhode Island. 1988.

BALLROOM

was designed by R.W. Scholes.
The typeface is Garamond ITC,
typeset by Stanton Publication Services,
and printed on 100 lb. Centura Gloss Text paper
by Diversified Graphics, Incorporated. The photographs
were scanned and printed as halftones, followed by
a dot-for-dot varnish process. The book was
Smythe sewn and perfect bound by Midwest Editions,
with a film laminate by American Laminating.

Ken Graves is the co-author of *American Snapshots*, a collection of amateur snapshots gathered from family albums (Scrimshaw Press, 1977). He was the recipient of a National Endowment for the Arts Fellowship in 1976 and 1986. His photography is in the collection of The Museum of Modern Art, The George Eastman House, and The National Library in Paris.

Born in Portland, Oregon, he earned a B.F.A. and M.F.A. in photography from the San Francisco Art Institute. At present, he is teaching photography at The Pennsylvania State University as an associate professor. The University has recently awarded him an Institute for the Arts and Humanistic Studies Fellowship to begin a photographic study of *The Nation of Children*, an orphanage of circus performers in Orense, Spain.

Photographs by Ken Graves appear on pages: 2, 16, 17, 18, 23, 24, 27, 29, 30, 35, 37, 38, 40, 41, 45, 49, 51, 53, 55, 56, 57, 58, 59, 60, 61, 63, 68, 70, 71, 73, 74, 75, 77, 78, 79, 80, 81, 83, 87, 88, 90, 91, 94, 95, 102, 103, 104, 106, 108, 112.

Eva Lipman was born in Czechoslovakia in 1946 and came to the U.S. with her family after the war. She grew up in New York City and earned a B.A. degree from Hunter College in literature, and an M.A. degree in social sciences from Columbia University. She lives and works in the city as a free-lance photographer and researcher. Her photographic essays have been exhibited in universities and New York City galleries.

Prior to meeting at a ballroom dance competition in Florida, Eva Lipman and Ken Graves were photographing this subject independently. Their respect for each others' photography developed into a collective effort. They are presently photographing boxing in inner city gymnasiums, continuing their visual exploration of subcultures in America.

Photographs by Eva Lipman appear on pages: 1, 13, 15, 19, 25, 26, 28, 31, 36, 39, 42, 43, 44, 50, 52, 54, 62, 67, 69, 72, 76, 89, 92, 93, 99, 100, 101, 105, 107, 109.

Miami Beach, Florida. 1987.